●sohotheatre

Setagaya Public Theatre and Soho 1

GW00360761

THE DIVER

by Hideki Noda and Colin Teevan

世田谷パブリックシアター
SETAGAYA PUBLIC THEATRE

First performed at Soho Theatre on 19 June 2008

Soho Theatre is supported by

  Bloomberg

Performances in the Lorenz Auditorium
Registered Charity No: 267234

Setagaya Public Theatre and Soho Theatre present

The Diver

by Hideki Noda and Colin Teevan

Cast

Harry Gostelow	**Genji and Prosecutor**
Kathryn Hunter	**Woman**
Hideki Noda	**Psychiatrist**
Glyn Pritchard	**Chief of Police and Tono Chujo**

The company also plays the roles of Emperor, Motel owner, Rokujo's men and Aoi's men.

Director	**Hideki Noda**
Composer	**Denzaemon Tanaka XIII**
Designer	**Catherine Chapman**
Lighting Designer	**Christoph Wagner**
Sound Designer	**Paul Arditti**
Assistant Director	**Ragga Dahl Johansen**
Noh Consultant	**Orpha Phelan**

For Soho Theatre

Production Manager	**Matt Noddings**
Company Stage Manager	**Dani Youngman**
Deputy Stage Manager	**Nina Scholar**
Assistant Stage Manager	**Natasha Emma Jones**
Wardrobe Supervisor	**Sydney Florence**
Technical Manager	**Nick Blount**
Head of Lighting	**Christoph Wagner**

For Setagaya Public Theatre

Director	**Hiromi Takatsuji**
Artistic Director	**Mansai Nomura**
Producer	**Chieko Hosaka**
Japanese Production Manager	**Sonoko Yamamoto**

The Diver

Acknowledgments

The Diver is the fourth play in a series of contemporary Noh plays. The idea for the series was devised by Mansai Nomura, Artistic Director of Setagaya Public Theatre.

Japanese traditional instruments (wa-gakki) are provided by Miyamoto Unosuke Co Ltd.

With thanks to the following for their English translations: Edward G Seidensticker for *Tale of Genji*; Ernest Fenollosa and Ezra Pound for *Lady Aoi*; and Shoichiro Kawai for *The Diver*.

With special thanks to Nadia Vawda and Spilios Argyropoulos.

Supported by the Agency for Cultural Affairs

SMBC
SUMITOMO MITSUI BANKING CORPORATION
EUROPE LIMITED

Evening sponsor,
London run

JAPANFOUNDATION

The Great Britain
SASAKAWA
FOUNDATION

Cast

Film includes *AKA, Shakespeare in Love* and *Shooting Fish*.

Harry Gostelow Genji and Prosecutor

Theatre includes *Pericles Prince of Tyre, King Lear, The Antipodes, Hamlet, The Comedy of Errors, Augustine's Oak, Man Falling Down* (Shakespeare's Globe), *The Importance of Being Earnest* (British Theatre Playhouse, Singapore and Greenwich), *Party Piece* (Theatre Royal Windsor/Tour), *Pinocchio* (Lyric Hammersmith), *Mr Puntila and his Man Matti* (Almeida/ Albery/Tour), *Ivanov* (Almeida/Moscow), *Measure for Measure* (Nottingham Playhouse/International Tour), *Run for your Wife, Out of Order, Pools Paradise, A Foot in the Door, How the Other Half Loves, Joking Apart, The Reluctant Debutante* (The Mill At Sonning), *Table Manners, The Public Eye* (Frinton Summer Theatre), *Scenes from Paradise* (Riverside Studios), *Forty Years On* (Stephen Joseph, Scarborough), *Richard III* (Ludlow Festival), *Murder at the Vicarage* (Theatre Royal Windsor/Richmond), *The Summer of the Eclipse* (Battersea Library), *Busy Body* (Battersea Bridge Lane), *Richard III* (Cliveden Festival).

Television includes *Miss Austen Regrets, After Thomas, EastEnders, Midsomer Murders, Foyle's War, Silent Witness, Breakout, Julia Jekyll & Harriet Hyde, The Bill, Soldier Soldier, Between the Lines* and *Class Act*.

Kathryn Hunter Woman

Directing includes *448 Psychosis* (LAMDA), *The Birds* by Aristophanes (National Theatre), T Bernhard's *Destination* (Volcano Theatre Company), Molière's *Wiseguy Scapino* (Theatre Clwyd), *Everyman* (RSC/BAM NY), *Mr Puntila and his man Matti* (Almeida/Albery/Traverse), *The Glory of Living* (Royal Court), *Comedy of Errors* and *Pericles* (Globe Theatre).

Acting includes: *Fragments* (directed by Peter Brook, Young Vic/Bouffes du Nord/world tour), *The Bee* (directed by Hideki Noda, Soho Theatre/Setagaya Theatre), *The Maids* (all three scripted roles, directed by Neil Bartlett, Brighton Festival), title role in *Yerma* (directed by Helena Kaut-Howson, Arcola Theatre), title role in *Celestina* (directed by Calixto Bieto, Birmingham/Edinburgh Festival), *Whistling Psyche* (directed by Robert Delamere, Almeida), title role in *Richard III* (directed by Barry Kyle, Globe Theatre), *The Taming of the Shrew* (directed by Phyllida Lloyd, Globe Theatre), *Dona Rosita* (directed by Phyllida Lloyd, Almeida), title role in *King Lear* (directed by Helena Kaut-Howson), Lady Macbeth in *Macbeth* (directed by Julia Bardsley) and *Electra* (directed by Nancy Meckler, Leicester Haymarket), Caryl Churchill's *Far Away* with Peter Brook (Bouffes du Nord, Paris), *The Rose Tattoo, The Devils* (Theatr Clywd), *Live*

Like Pigs (directed by Katie Mitchell), *The Recruiting Officer* (directed by Max Stafford Clark), *Our Country's Good* (Royal Court Theatre), *The Hypochondriac* (Leicester/Lyric/Haymarket), *Women of Troy* (Gate), *Romeo and Juliet* (Watermill), *Spoonface Steinberg* (directed by Annie Castledine & Marcello Magni, Ambassadors/Washington), *Mother Courage* (Shared Experience/Ambassadors/Spoletto Festival/South Carolina), *Pericles* and *The Visit* (Olivier Award for Best Actress, National Theatre), *The Skriker* (Time Out Award for Best Actress and Olivier Nomination for Best Actress, National Theatre). Work for Theatre de Complicite includes *Foe, Out of the House Walked a Man* (directed by Simon McBurney), *The Visit* (National Theatre), *Anything for a Quiet Life, Help, I am Alive!* and *The Winter's Tale*.

Film includes: *Harry Potter and the order of the Phoenix*, Mike Leigh's *All or Nothing, Wet and Dry*, Sally Potter's *Orlando* and Peter Greenaway's *Baby of Macon*.

Television includes: *Rome, Silent Witness, CSI: Manhunt, Grushko* and *Maria's Child* (BBC).

Hideki Noda Co-writer, Director and roles of Psychiatrist/Aoi

Hideki Noda is a prolific writer, director, and actor. His work has had a huge influence on Japanese Theatre, and he has long been acclaimed as a leading theatre practitioner.

Hideki was born in 1955 in Nagasaki, Japan. He established the theatre company Yume no Yuminsha whilst at Tokyo University in 1976. He went on to study theatre in London and, in 1993, established the theatre company NODA MAP.

Hideki's recent theatre credits as writer/director/actor include *The Bee* (Japan/Soho Theatre, London), *Red Demon* (Young Vic, London/Japan/Thailand/ Korea), *Oil, Kill, Pandora's Bell, Under the Cherry Blossom, Half God, Descent of the Brutes* (Edinburgh Lyceum Theatre/Japan), *A Messenger from the Comet* (BAM, New York, /Japan), *The Tragedy of Togitatsu* and *Nezumi Kozo* (his original versions of the classical Kabuki piece at Kabuki Theatre). Recent credits as writer/director include *The Opera Macbeth* (New National Theatre, Japan).

Hideki has won most of the major drama awards in Japan. Hideki will be Artistic Director of the Tokyo Metropolitan Theatre in 2009.

Glyn Pritchard Chief of Police/Tono Chujo

Theatre includes *Under Milk Wood* (Tricycle Theatre), *A Family Affair* (Arcola Theatre), *Hard Times, Accidental Death of an Anarchist* (Theatr Clwyd), *Abigail's Party* (Millford Haven), *The Last Minute* (Stephen Norrington), *Neville's Island* (Torch Theatre, Millford Haven),

King Lear (Young Vic and Far East tour), *The Bee* (Soho Theatre), *Under Milk Wood, Blue Remembered Hills* (The Dukes, Lancaster), *King Lear* (Haymarket Theatre Leicester), *Body Talk* (Royal Court), *The Fairy Queen* (Northern Symphonia), *Full Moon* (The Young Vic/Theatr Clwyd), *Ghetto, Fuente Ovejuna* and *Bartholomew Fair* (National Theatre).

Film and television includes *A470, The Bill, V Graith, Animal Ark, Y Glas, Butterflies, Brookside, Dirty Work, Brides of War, Famous Five, Coronation Street, Balance of Power, A Mind to Kill, Natural Justice/Dial, Pobol Y Cwm, Ruth Rendell, Paper Mask, Death of a Son, Butterfles* (short film) and *Lion* (short film).

Company

Colin Teevan Co-Writer

Colin Teevan was born in Dublin. His recent stage work includes *How Many Miles to Basra?* (West Yorkshire Playhouse, winner of 2007 Clarion Award for Best New Play), *The Bee*, co-written with Hideki Noda, (Soho Theatre/ Setagaya Theatre,Tokyo), *Missing Persons, Four Tragedies and Roy Keane* (Assembly Rooms, Edinburgh/Trafalgar Studios) *Alcmaeon in Corinth* (Newcastle Live!), *Monkey* (The Young Vic/ Dundee Rep; upcoming at West Yorkshire Playhouse and Polka Theatre), *The Walls*, (National Theatre), *Vinegar and Brown Paper* (Abbey, Dublin) *The Big*

Sea (Galloglass Ireland/Riverside Studios).

Stage adaptations include Ibsen's *Peer Gynt* (National Theatre of Scotland and Dundee Rep), *Don Quixote* adapted from Cervantes with Pablo Ley (West Yorkshire Playhouse), *Svejk*, from the novel by Jaroslav Hasek (Gate London/ The Duke, New York).

Stage translations include *Bacchai* by Euripides (National Theatre/ Epidaurus, Greece) and *Cuckoos* by Giuseppe Manfridi (Gate/Barbican), both directed by Sir Peter Hall, *Marathon* by Edoardo Erba (Gate London, upcoming at Assembly Rooms Edinburgh) and *Iph...*, a version of Euripides' *Iphigeneia in Aulis* (Lyric, Belfast/Mercury Colchester).

Radio plays include *Iph..., Tricycles, The RoyKeaneiad Parts 1 and 2, Medea: The Last Word, Arse, The Revanant, How Many Miles to Basra?, The Devil Was Here Yesterday*, all BBC Radio 3 and *Glass Houses,* and *Myrrha* BBC Radio 4.

As well as working on new plays for West Yorkshire Playhouse, Dundee Rep and the Tricycle, Colin is currently collaborating on a new one-woman show with Kathryn Hunter and Walter Meierjohann for the Young Vic. While in August he will be directing his own play *Alcmaeon in Corinth* for the National Theatre Bitola, Macedonia in August.

He was the production dramaturg and associate director on Sir Peter Hall's *Tantalus* (RSC/

Denver Center for Performing Arts). He was writer-in-residence at Queen's University, Belfast; Screen East Writing Fellow at UEA and North Eastern Literary Fellow based at the Universities of Newcastle and Durham. He is currently lecturer in dramatic writing at the University of Newcastle and has recently become an associate artist at West Yorkshire Playhouse.

All his work is published by Oberon Books.

Denzaemon Tanaka XIII
Composer

The 13th maestro for KABUKI music, Denzaemon Tanaka XIII was born in 1976. He is the second son of leading Noh musician Kamei Tadao, and the 12th maestro for Kabuki music Tanaka Sataro.

Having trained since the age of two, Denzaemon made his Noh and Kabuki music debut at five, and his debut in Kabuki-za theatre in 1990. In 1993, aged 16, he was chosen specifically as the youngest concert master in the 400-year history of the Kabuki tradition. In 2004, at the performance of *Ibaragi* by Bando Tamasaburo, he became maestro Tanaka Denzaemon XIII.

He has since worked on many new Kabuki dance and theatre compositions, and participated in various overseas performances in the Opéra de Paris in Paris, the Met in New York, the National Theatre in London, as well as work in China, Korea, Italy, Sweden and Germany.

Currently he leads *Sankyo-Kai* for both Noh and Kabuki, with his elder brother Kamei Hirotada and his younger brother Tanaka Denjiro.

Catherine Chapman
Designer

Catherine Chapman trained in Theatre Design at Nottingham Trent University and graduated in 2003.

Recent production designs include: *Fly in the Ointment, Cover her Feet (*Stephen Joseph Theatre), *1984, Keys to the Kingdom, Bouncers, September in the Rain, The Trial*, *The Hunchback of Notre Dame* (York Theatre Royal), *The Girl who Lost her Smile* (Tutti Frutti), *Madame Butterfly* (English National Opera Education).

Catherine works extensively with young people including youth theatre, community projects and working as an artist in schools.

Christoph Wagner
Lighting Designer

Christoph Wagner is currently Head of Lighting at Soho Theatre. He has previously worked with Hideki Noda re-lighting Rick Fisher's original design for *The Bee* at Setagaya Theatre, Tokyo. Designs for Soho include *The Tiger Lillies – Seven Deadly Sins, Moonwalking in Chinatown, Thom Pain (based on nothing)*, *How to Act around Cops, How To Lose Friends and Alienate People* and numerous cabaret and comedy shows. Other past designs include

Bitches Ball (Hoxton Hall, touring), *House* (Finborough Theatre), *Risk* (Actors' Centre), *Perfect* (touring), *Robin Hood* (Riverside Studios) and various corporate events.

Paul Arditti Sound Designer

Recent designs include *The Revenger's Tragedy, Never So Good, Happy Now, Saint Joan* (National Theatre), *The Year of Magical Thinking* (National Theatre, London/ Booth Theatre, Broadway, NY), *Les Liaisons Dangereuses* (American Airlines Theatre, Broadway, NY), *Billy Elliot The Musical* (Capitol Theatre, Sydney/Victoria Palace Theatre, London), *The Member of the Wedding, Vernon God Little, The Respectable Wedding* (Young Vic), *Nakamitsu* (Gate Theatre), *The Pain and the Itch* (Royal Court), *Hergé's Adventures of Tintin* (Barbican Theatre/Playhouse Theatre).

Awards and nominations include *Saint Joan* (Olivier Award for Best Sound Design 2008), *Billy Elliot The Musical* (Olivier Award for Best Sound Design 2006), *Festen* (Evening Standard Award for Best Design 2005, Olivier Award nomination for Best Sound Design 2005), *The Pillowman* (Drama Desk Award for Outstanding Sound Design 2005, Olivier Award nomination for Best Sound Design 2004), *Crestfall* (Irish Times Theatre Awards nomination Judges' Special Award 2004), *Far Away* (Lucille Lortel Award nomination 2004), *The Chairs* (Drama Desk Award nomination for Outstanding Sound Design 2003) and *Four Baboons Adoring the Sun* (Drama Desk Award for Outstanding Sound Design 1993).

Ragga Dahl Johansen
Assistant Director

Ragga is artistic director of Ginnungagap Teaterkompani.

Her work as an assistant director includes *The Bee* (Soho Theatre), *4.48 Psychosis* (LAMDA), *Timon of Athens* (RADA), *Two* (BAC) and *Three More Sleepless Nights* (BAC).

As a director, her work includes *Nansens Sønn* (Tromsø, Norway), *Story of Phillip* (Tromsø, Norway, Helsinki, Finland, Peacock Theatre), *Traffic Light* (Shakespeare's Globe @ Balham), *Notes on Falling Leaves* (BAC) and *Hippo Love* (BAC).

Ragga also works as a freelance youth drama workshop leader.

● soho theatre

performance	provocative and compelling theatre, comedy and cabaret
talks	vibrant debates on culture, the arts and the way we live
soho connect	a thriving learning, community and outreach programme
writers' centre	discovering and nurturing new writers and artists
soho theatre bar	serving tasty, affordable food and drink from 12pm till late

'The capital's centre for daring international drama.' Evening Standard
'London's coolest theatre by a mile' Midweek

21 Dean Street
London W1D 3NE
Admin: 020 7287 5060
Box Office: 020 7478 0100
sohotheatre.com

Soho Theatre online
Giving you the latest information and previews of upcoming shows, Soho Theatre can be found on facebook, myspace and youtube as well as at sohotheatre.com

For regular programme updates and offers visit sohotheatre.com/mailing

Hiring the theatre
Soho Theatre has a range of rooms and spaces for hire. Please contact the theatre on 020 7287 5060 or go to sohotheatre.com/hires for further details.

The Terrace Bar
Drinks can be taken into the auditorium and are available from the Terrace Bar on the second floor.

● soho theatre

THE SOHO THEATRE DEVELOPMENT CAMPAIGN

Soho Theatre receives core funding from Arts Council England, London.

In order to provide as diverse a programme as possible and expand our audience development and outreach work, we rely upon additional support from trusts, foundations, individuals and businesses. All of our major sponsors share a common commitment to developing new areas of activity and encouraging creative partnerships between business and the arts. We are immensely grateful for the invaluable support from our sponsors and donors and wish to thank them for their continued commitment.

Soho Theatre has a Friends Scheme in support of its education programme and work developing new writers and reaching new audiences. To find out how to become a Friend of Soho Theatre, contact the development department on 020 7478 0109, email development@sohotheatre.com or visit sohotheatre.com.

Sponsors:
Angels, The Costumiers, Bloomberg, TEQUILA\London, Rathbones

Principal Supporters and Education Patrons:
Anonymous
The City Bridge Trust
The Ernest Cook Trust
Tony and Rita Gallagher
Nigel Gee
The Paul Hamlyn Foundation
Roger Jospé
Jack and Linda Keenan
John Lyon's Charity
Man Group plc Charitable Trust
Sigrid Rausing
The Rose Foundation
Carolyn Ward
The Harold Hyam Wingate Foundation

Soho Supporting Partner:
Goodman Derrick

Soho Business Members:
The Groucho Club
Ronnie Scott's Jazz Club

Trusts and Foundations:
Anonymous
The Carr-Gregory Trust
The Great Britain Sasakawa Foundation
Miss Hazel Wood Charitable Trust

Hyde Park Place Estate Charity
The Kobler Trust
The Mackintosh Foundation
Teale Charitable Trust

Belarus Free Theatre Campaign:
Anonymous
Anglo-Belarusian Society
Alan Bennett
Count Andrew Ciechanowiecki
Caryl Churchill
Richard Curtis
Michael Frayn
Jenny Hall
David Heyman
Nicholas Hytner
Emma Thompson
Alan Rickman

Dear Friends:
Anonymous
Jill and Michael Barrington
David Day
John Drummond
Madeleine Hamel
Norma Heyman
Jane and Andrew McManus
Michael and Mimi Naughton
Hannah Pierce
Nicola Stanhope
Alex Vogel

Good Friends and Friends:
Thank you also to the many Soho Friends we are unable to list here.

For a full list of our patrons, please visit sohotheatre.com

Registered Charity: 267234

世田谷パブリックシアター
SETAGAYA PUBLIC THEATRE

Setagaya Public Theatre is a non-profit theatre funded by the
city of Setagaya, the second largest borough in central Tokyo.
Since its opening in 1997, Setagaya has become highly acclaimed
for producing theatre in Japan. Setagaya Public Theatre runs two
theatres, the Main Theatre and the Theatre Tram. Its aim is both to
produce and present major national and international contemporary
drama and dance.

Setagaya Public Theatre is also known to co-produce top-notch
international collaborative projects such as *The Elephant Vanishes*
(Tokyo, Osaka, London, New York, Paris and Michigan in 2003 and
2004) and *Shun-kin* (Tokyo, London 2008 and 09) with Simon
McBurney, *Asobu* with Jeseph Nadi (Tokyo, Avignon and other cities
in 2006 and 07) and *Screens* and *Seoul Citizen* with a French director
Fredric Fisbach (Tokyo, Paris, Avignon in 2002, 2003, 2004, 2006
and 2007), *Andersen Project* – Japanese version with Robert Lepage
(Tokyo and domestic tours in 2006) and many other collaborative
productions with Asian artists. Mansai Nomura has been Artistic
Director since 2002.

For *The Diver*:
Producer   Chieko Hosaka
Tokyo Production Manager   Sonoko Yamamoto
Artistic Director   Mansai Nomura

Foreword to The Diver

Hideki Noda in conversation with Nina Steiger

After our successful production of *The Bee* at Soho Theatre in the summer of 2006, our team was excited to collaborate on another production and to continue exploring the Japanese stylization of Noh and Kabuki, which, in that show, had been so interesting to Western audiences. There was an appreciation of each other's processes as I had worked with Colin and the cast, particularly Kathryn Hunter. After three preliminary workshops, the story was eventually structured and Colin was able to begin scripting.

Our production of *The Diver* draws on three sets of source material: the first is a Noh play called *Ama*, which translates as 'Pearl Diver Woman' in Japanese. The second one is the *Tale of Genji*, a classical Japanese novel written in 1008, just a thousand years ago by a Japanese noblewoman, Murasaki Shikibu. It is a clever, poetic and fantastic novel, which tells the story of Genji, the son of the emperor and a low-ranking concubine and it forms the basis of several important Noh plays. I had read the Genji Tales as a high school student and found it a difficult text as its complex grammar and language are from the Heian period court Japanese. The third piece of source material is a real criminal case, which held a remarkable resonance with the two older texts.

The Noh stylization is the simplest imaginable, conveying an intense internal energy with an extremely still, spare physical language. To explore the world of the Noh play we looked at one called *Aoi no Ue* (*Lady Aoi*) by Zeami, an actor and writer who lived and performed in 14th and 15th centuries. It tells the story of Genji, his wife Lady Aoi and mistress, Lady Rokujo. It is an intense and passionate story but in order to fully understand the world of this play, we needed to look at the Genji Tales on which it is based.

So as an ensemble, we studied this episode of jealousy and possession in the Tales and we became very interested in the characters and stories, in particular, the love and jealousy in the relationship between Aoi and Rokujo, the revenge tragedy and the notion of a wandering spirit. As we worked with the Noh play and the Genji Tales, we found the stories contemporary and compelling. As with *The Bee*, there is an implicit connection with today's society, its values and aesthetics but in these Tales, we felt there was still a space for something else. And this led me to a modern criminal case in which a young woman was driven to murder, compelled by similar emotions to those that motivate the characters in the Genji story.

After World War II, the way of thinking in Japan changed, relating less to philosophy and religion and instead, focusing on the pursuit of economic growth and the trends of US culture. It occurs to me that we lost a more symbolic, abstracted way of thinking.

Recently, in Japan, especially among the youth, there has been a growing interest in areas like fortune-telling and past lives, seeking answers and creating belief systems based on superstition. For instance, many people in

Japan now believe that blood type carries information about your character and personality and even, your future. Still, in some way, this is a return to thinking about spirits and destiny that is the central focus of the Genji Tales and Noh drama. Partly through the blending of Eastern and Western traditions and ancient and modern texts, we can re-connect the stories from the distant past to modern trends and convictions.

I'm really interested in ancient belief. In the past, it was thought that the spirit was connected to one's own culture. Today as well, people need to be able to trace the connections between their lives and the sense of a wider social history. In *The Diver*, the Psychiatrist helps the Woman to understand who she is and where she comes from by exploring the links between her own story and the culture and civilisation of the past. Nevertheless, this is a complicated process and the play attempts to express some of the difficulties of understanding another person's mentality, not to mention the challenges of understanding a different culture.

The development of our script depends hugely on its physical life which we are discovering in rehearsal every day; we are constantly making adjustments, looking for lines that explain too much and scenes that are too overt. I believe good theatre resists the urge to explain too much; the theatrical imagination can understand things that are implied through action, suggestion, image, gesture, simplicity. This is the essence of Noh style and it is the opposite of the television culture today, which provides you with everything. By leaving things out or letting physicality, style and tone tell the story, we involve the audience as they stretch their imaginations.

In our production, the process is unusual, ambiguous and very important as a journey. At the moment, we have the ending of the play written but we still don't feel we fully understand it. In the Eastern tradition, this uncertainty is essential to the process. However, when I work in Tokyo with Japanese actors, I always tell them to make it clear, not to be too ambiguous. I'm always thinking about the border between Eastern and Western ways of thinking. Even for a Japanese ensemble, the Noh plays are highly complex and ambiguous. For our ensemble and in making *The Diver*, the process has been to find a balance between the poetic intensity of these ancient stories and the timeless values and images at their heart.

THE DIVER

First published in 2008 by Oberon Books Ltd
521 Caledonian Road, London N7 9RH
Tel: 020 7607 3637 / Fax: 020 7607 3629
e-mail: info@oberonbooks.com
www.oberonbooks.com

A catalogue record for this book is available from the British
Library.

ISBN: 978-1-84002-8683

Cover image: Yuki Sawaga.

Cover Photos: Sheila Burnett and Nadia Vawda

Printed in Great Britain by CPI Antony Rowe, Chippenham.

Characters

PSYCHIATRIST

WOMAN

PROSECUTOR

CHIEF OF POLICE

Other roles played by the four protagonists

EMPEROR

DRAGON QUEEN

GENJI

BOAT MEN

TONOCHUJO

MOTEL OWNER

AOI'S MEN

ROKUJO'S MEN

AOI

The text that follows was used for the production at Soho Theatre on 19 June 2008 and was correct at the time of going to press.

Scene 1

A Police Station Tokyo.

A Consultation Room.

Enter PSYCHIATRIST. He opens a book and makes notes. He becomes engrossed in the book. The book becomes a mask.

WOMAN is led by guard through police station to Consultation Room.

Scene 2

WOMAN enters Consultation Room. Guard removes the handcuffs. Exit guard.

Long silence.

PSYCHIATRIST
So, what should I call you today?

WOMAN does not respond. Silence.

The Observation Room. CHIEF OF POLICE and PROSECUTOR observe the PSYCHIATRIST and WOMAN.

CHIEF OF POLICE
The public demand justice,
The public are outraged.

PROSECUTOR
We all want to see justice done, Inspector.

CHIEF OF POLICE
So?

PROSECUTOR
So?

CHIEF OF POLICE
So where's the problem, Your Honour?

PROSECUTOR
There is none.

CHIEF OF POLICE
So let us charge and try her.

PROSECUTOR
You have proof, Inspector?

CHIEF OF POLICE
She is all the proof we need.

PROSECUTOR
You are Police Chief of the Prefecture,
I the District Prosecutor,
I will decide when we have proof enough.

The Consultation Room.

PSYCHIATRIST
So, if you won't tell me who you are,
Then tell me what you're doing?

WOMAN
I'm catching the moon on the surface of the sea.

PSYCHIATRIST
And we are where today?

WOMAN
Sanuki Province at Shido Bay.

The Observation Room.

CHIEF OF POLICE
Hours after the blast the suspect was found
Wandering the streets of Fuchu City, her hand
Burnt and raw, her clothes
Blackened by flames.

PROSECUTOR
Circumstantial evidence.

CHIEF OF POLICE
It makes sense.

PROSECUTOR
She does not remember who she is.

The Consultation Room.

PSYCHIATRIST
Do you know who I am?

WOMAN
Of course, you are the Emperor's son.

The Observation Room.

CHIEF OF POLICE
So what if she does not remember who she is?

PROSECUTOR
It shows she was not in her right mind, at the very least.

CHIEF OF POLICE

She's putting it on,

She can't face up to what she's done.

PROSECUTOR

Perhaps,

Or perhaps it's a case of dissociation.

Whatever it may be, in this nation

A person is innocent until proven guilty,

That is why I have appointed

An expert in criminal psychology.

The Consultation Room.

PSYCHIATRIST

So I am the Emperor's son,

What am I doing here in Shido Bay?

WOMAN

It was here, so you were told in a dream,

Your honoured mother passed away.

PSYCHIATRIST

My mother?

WOMAN

And so you've come

To pray for her soul, that it might find peace.

PSYCHIATRIST

The souls of both the living and dead

Must find peace. That is why I'm here.

Silence.

Observation Room.

CHIEF OF POLICE
A psychiatrist to tell us what's as plain
As the noses on our faces!

PROSECUTOR
He will assess the suspect, then hand his report in.

CHIEF OF POLICE
He's been with her every day since she was brought in,
What progress has he made?
Give her to me for an hour she'll soon remember
Who she is, she'll soon confess
To what she's done.

PROSECUTOR
The psychiatrist is the one
Who must decide that.
We must wait and see what he says.

CHIEF OF POLICE
The public demand justice,
The public are outraged.
And we can hold a suspect
For only twenty-three days.
We're wasting time.

PROSECUTOR
The public shall just have to wait.

CHIEF OF POLICE
I'll see her swinging from a rope for this.

PROSECUTOR
And what if she were your daughter?

CHIEF OF POLICE
I have no daughter.

PROSECUTOR
I do, and justice, Inspector,
Is all I want to see.

The Consultation Room.

PSYCHIATRIST
Why are you trying to catch the moon
On the surface of the sea?

WOMAN
Why shouldn't I?

PSYCHIATRIST
Because it's an impossibility.

WOMAN
We all yearn for impossible treasures.

PSYCHIATRIST
Do we?

WOMAN
The treasures that you seek
Lie upon the ocean's bed.

PSYCHIATRIST
What treasure am I seeking?

WOMAN
The priceless jewel stolen by the Dragon Queen.

PSYCHIATRIST
What jewel?

WOMAN
The jewel that never turns away.

PSYCHIATRIST
When was it stolen?

WOMAN
When you were just a little boy.

PSYCHIATRIST
I see.

Enter EMPEROR.

WOMAN
And when your father the Emperor returned to Shido Bay,
He asked the pearl diver
To retrieve the lost treasure…

EMPEROR
Fetch me the jewel from the bottom of the sea.

WOMAN
If I do what you ask of me,
You must swear you'll safeguard our son.

EMPEROR
I will protect and honour him.

Scene 3

WOMAN

So, though it might cost me my life,

I'll do it for our son.

I'll take my sharp-edged knife

And wrap around my waist

A rope a thousand fathoms long.

And if I wrest from the Dragon Queen

The jewel that never turns away,

I'll give the rope a pull

And you, without delay, must all haul me back up.

And without looking back I leap,

And dive –

WOMAN dives into the sea.

And sky becomes sea,

And clouds waves,

And down, down, down I go into the rolling deep.

And there, upon the ocean-bed I see

A jade tower, three hundred metres high,

Where the Dragon Queen lies asleep,

The precious jewel clasped in her claw.

How can I who have no magic power

Hope to succeed?

And what of my child?

I shall never see him again.

I cannot bear the pain of parting.

Press the blade of mercy to your forehead,

And charge, charge, charge the deadly dragon's lair.

WOMAN charges the Dragon Queen and steals the jewel. She is pursued by the Dragon Queen. WOMAN cuts herself beneath the breast, hides the jewel in the wound and pulls upon the rope.

EMPEROR
Pull hard, men!

WOMAN is hauled to surface, apparently dead.

The broken, bloodied body of the diver:
The precious jewel is lost forever.

WOMAN gasps.

WOMAN
Look carefully, beneath my breast.

EMPEROR
A wound. And there, within it,
Glows the radiant jewel.

WOMAN dies.

PSYCHIATRIST
Who are you?

WOMAN
I am that diver's ghost.
Now I must go back under the sea –

WOMAN goes to exit.

Scene 4

The Consultation Room. Enter CHIEF OF POLICE.

PSYCHIATRIST

Inspector, you cannot burst unannounced
Into my consultation room!

CHIEF OF POLICE

You'll soon see if I can or I cannot.
What's this, Yumi Yamanaka?

Pause.

Recognise it? Look, you're shaking like maraca.

PSYCHIATRIST

Inspector, you are undoing all the progress we were
making.

CHIEF OF POLICE

Progress! This is progress?
A lighter just like this was found
On the ground outside the apartment,
Her fingerprints upon it.
What's wrong, Yamanaka?
Cat got your tongue?

CHIEF OF POLICE lights lighter under her nose.

She flinched, you saw it,
The glint of recognition in her eyes.

PSYCHIATRIST

It was fear, because you nearly burnt her face.

CHIEF OF POLICE
Admit it, Miss Yamanaka,
It's your only hope of avoiding the death sentence.

Pause.

WOMAN
I'm sorry, but I'm not this Miss Yamanaka.

CHIEF OF POLICE
Who are you then?

Beat.

WOMAN
The Emperor's mistress.

PSYCHIATRIST
The Diver.

WOMAN
No, I am the Emperor's favourite mistress.
A lady of slightly inferior rank, perhaps,
But a lady all the same.
I am The Emperor's true wife in all but name –

CHIEF OF POLICE
The Emperor's favourite mistress?
Well in that case, I'm so sorry, Your Highness.
(*To PSYCHIATRIST.*) Progress?

WOMAN
And the Emperor will soon hear of this –

CHIEF OF POLICE
(*To WOMAN.*) I'm onto you, I've got your number.

(*To PSYCHIATRIST.*) And if you can't make her remember
Who she is and what she's done, I soon will.
I'll tell the press of this new evidence, the lighter,
They'll demand we charge and try her.

Exit CHIEF OF POLICE.

WOMAN
He loves me more than any of his other wives
He insists I'm always at his side.
His wives despise me, especially
Since I gave birth to our son.
A child of such perfect beauty,
He hardly seems meant for this sad world.
The Emperor calls him his secret treasure.
It's clear he gives him more pleasure
Than any other of his other sons,
Even the crown prince.
But since his wives are so consumed with jealousy,
He's given him a commoner's name: Genji.

A telephone rings.

(*Greatly disturbed.*) I'm sorry! I'm sorry! I'm so sorry!

PSYCHIATRIST
Why are you sorry… Yumi?

Silence.

PSYCHIATRIST
Yumi? Yumi? Is that you?

WOMAN
Who?

Who is this Yumi?

It was the wives, their jealousy,

That's why soon after Genji's birth I fell ill,

And the Emperor he knew I was the victim of some curse
  or spell.

And as the dew slips from the leaf,

I slipped softly from this earth

And died.

Pause. WOMAN slips from sofa.

PSYCHIATRIST

You died?

WOMAN

Last year's blossoms

Are but a dream of the mind.

PSYCHIATRIST

So I am talking to a dead person?

WOMAN

Is that so odd?

PSYCHIATRIST

I can't say it's every day

I converse with the dead.

Do you know why you're here Miss…?

The CHIEF OF POLICE appears flicking lighter.

WOMAN

I lost my lighter, the angry man said.

Pause.

PSYCHIATRIST

And I'm afraid our time is up.

We must stop, for today at least.

WOMAN

Can I ask you a question?

PSYCHIATRIST

By all means.

WOMAN

Do you believe the soul of a person lost in grief

Can wander off all by itself?

Door is opened, wind is heard.

PSYCHIATRIST (*Into recorder.*)

End of session three.

Subject continues to shift identity:

Pearl diver's ghost, Emperor's favourite mistress…

Genji? Genji? Name rings a bell.

Scene 5

Consultation Room. Enter CHIEF OF POLICE and PROSECUTOR.

CHIEF OF POLICE

So, Doctor, how far have you got?

PROSECUTOR

Does she remember who she is or not?

PSYCHIATRIST

Your Honour, Inspector,

I believe we've made a breakthrough.

CHIEF OF POLICE
A breakthrough?

PROSECUTOR
Good. (*To CHIEF OF POLICE.*) You see?

PSYCHIATRIST
Genji.

CHIEF OF POLICE
What?

PSYCHIATRIST
The first novel written in Japanese.

PROSECUTOR
The eleventh century.
Some believe it to be the first novel in world literature.

CHIEF OF POLICE
Fascinating, I'm sure.
I'm sorry, but I thought I heard you say
That you had made a breakthrough.

PSYCHIATRIST
The name. Yesterday.
The Emperor's dead mistress' son:
Genji.

PROSECUTOR's mobile rings.

She plays –

PROSECUTOR
Excuse me while I take this call.
Yes? Yes, hi. No, all's well –

PSYCHIATRIST
She plays characters from this story –

CHIEF OF POLICE
Plays?

PSYCHIATRIST
Believes.

CHIEF OF POLICE
Believes she's characters in a story from the eleventh
  century?
Are you having a laugh?

PROSECUTOR
I too wish I was with you in the bath.

CHIEF OF POLICE
How is that meant to help our case?

PROSECUTOR
My hand?

CHIEF OF POLICE
Her name is Yumi. Yumi! Yumi!

PROSECUTOR
It's on your tummy. The other one?

*CHIEF OF POLICE and PSYCHIATRIST look at
PROSECUTOR.*

(*Sotto.*) Is dropping down, down, down into the deep

Bath water.

Yes…yes I'll tell her tonight.

(*To the others.*) Sorry gentlemen, my daughter.

(*To phone.*) I'm still at work. We'll talk later.

CHIEF OF POLICE

As I was saying, her name is Yumi Yamanaka,

An assistant in systems information

At the JEC Corporation.

She was having an affair with a systems engineer,

Sachio Sasaki,

And it was she who set fire –

Enter WOMAN.

CHIEF OF POLICE

Gentlemen, the Emperor's mistress!

WOMAN

Me? Good heavens no.

Scene 6

Interrogation Room. WOMAN and CHIEF OF POLICE.

CHIEF OF POLICE

So,

Who are you then?

You must forgive me, Miss…

But you see with cutbacks in the precinct

Money spent on psychiatrists and such things,

There's little left for basic policing.

So when it comes to the good-cop/bad-cop routine

I must play them all, it seems.

So Miss…?

Perhaps you'd help me with this problem,

One with which I have been grappling:

A corpse is found

Covered in blood,

Decapitated,

The severed head lying on the ground,

Several feet away,

And over the corpse stands

A man with a bloody axe in his hand.

Now what do you think the likely cause of death?

Do you think it's A: an accident?

B: death by misadventure?

C: perhaps it's suicide?

Or do you think our friend there with the axe?

Do you think he might have had a hand in it?

I'm asking you.

I'M ASKING YOU!

You see the problem that I'm having?

A fire, two dead,

Your lighter found at the scene?

See what I mean?

SEE WHAT I MEAN?

Talk to me Yumi.

We can only hold you for thirteen more days.

We will charge you regardless,

Have no fear on that score,

So why not just admit who you are

And what you've done?

It's your only chance of avoiding the drop,

Of not being hanged by your neck
From the end of a rope.
Say! Say, Yumi, who are you?

   WOMAN (*Shaking.*)
Evening Faces.

   CHIEF OF POLICE
Evening Faces?

   WOMAN (*Shaking.*)
Evening Faces.

Scene 7

The Consultation Room.

   PSYCHIATRIST
Evening Faces. Chapter Four.
(*Indicating book.*) Genji's affair with Evening Faces.
So you now are his lover?

   WOMAN
I will be your guardian in this world and the other.
I love him and he loves me. He chose this dress for me.
For my birthday. The seventh of July.

   PSYCHIATRIST
So where did you meet your Genji?
At work perhaps?
Or at a bar in Fuchu City?

   WOMAN
No, no, I met him in the evening light.

Scene 8

A flower grows.

WOMAN
Where in the world can I call home?
This earth is a temporary shelter,
I have always been alone.

Enter GENJI.

GENJI
Lady, what is that flower,
So white in the golden evening light?

An exchange of messages on fans.

WOMAN
That flower is known as Evening Faces,
It blooms from the cracks in deserted places.

GENJI
An unfortunate sort of flower,
To bloom in such a place at such an hour.

WOMAN
Yet one that has the power to thrive
On so little sustenance.

GENJI
And you, what sustenance
Do you require to stay alive?

WOMAN
A little light, a little nourishment,
Some warmth, is all the encouragement I need.

GENJI

(*To WOMAN.*) And I've no need to ask your name;
So beautiful a white face,
Blooming in the evening twilight
In this deserted place.

A boat. Fireworks.

Happy birthday, Evening Faces,
I organised them specially for you.

BOATMEN

Happy Tanabata!

GENJI and WOMAN look at fireworks.

Even people who were nothing to him
Were drawn to Genji. Rough mountain men
Would pause under the shade of the cherry tree,
To admire him. And those who'd basked,
However briefly in his radiance,
Were filled with thoughts, each in accordance
With his rank, of course, of how
They might be of service to him;
Offering up their daughter to him as a servant –

GENJI lays stepping stones upon the water.

GENJI

Or a not unpretty sister for my private pleasures.

WOMAN

It's not surprising then that people of some sensibility,
Who had upon some occasion
Received perhaps a piece of poetry,
Or some other kindness,

Found him much on their minds.

And it distressed them not to be always with him.

(*To GENJI.*)

Let us make our wishes and hang them on the tree.

GENJI

What did you wish for?

WOMAN

You, forever. And you?

GENJI

Same. Me forever too.

He laughs.

I'm joking, of course.

GENJI's mobile rings. The spell is broken.

Scene 9

Consultation Room.

PSYCHIATRIST

And that was your first time?

WOMAN

First time?

PSYCHIATRIST

The first time…you had intercourse?

WOMAN

No. You asked me how we met.

PSYCHIATRIST
But your first time?

WOMAN (*Confused.*)
I don't remember.

PSYCHIATRIST
This Genji, your Genji, what does he do?

WOMAN
Do?

PSYCHIATRIST
Work.

WOMAN
Nothing.

PSYCHIATRIST
But how does he live?

WOMAN
Very well. He's famous, I said.

PSYCHIATRIST
But what's he famous for?

WOMAN
For being the Emperor's son.

PSYCHIATRIST
By his mistress?

WOMAN
His favourite mistress.

PSYCHIATRIST
What's he like?

WOMAN
He's beautiful.
A man of such perfect beauty,
He hardly seems meant for this sad world.
He chose this dress for me.

PSYCHIATRIST
When?

WOMAN
The first time we…

PSYCHIATRIST
Had intercourse?

WOMAN
The first time we crossed the line.

PSYCHIATRIST
Where was this, Yumi… Evening Faces?

WOMAN
Celebrity *Perfect Ten*.

PSYCHIATRIST
Celebrity *Perfect Ten*?

Scene 10

WOMAN
Yes, *Perfect Ten*, on Wowow,
Every Wednesday at ten pm.

You must know it.

And each year they do one with celebrities,

For charity –

WOMAN watches Perfect Ten *on television.*

V/O

Ladies and Gentlemen it's the *Perfect Ten* Show,

And here's your host To-no-chu-jo!

Applause.

TONOCHUJO

Good evening, good evening…listen to you!

Applause.

Welcome to Celebrity *Perfect Ten*

The show where real men

Get to build themselves the babes of their dreams

So let's see which celebrity

Is behind tonight's wet dream settee.

Enter GENJI.

Good evening, good evening, and what's you're name?

GENJI

Genji.

TONOCHUJO

And what do you do?

GENJI

Nothing, I'm the son of the mistress of the Emperor.

Applause.

TONOCHUJO
Listen to him!

GENJI
Listen to me!

TONOCHUJO
Don't steal my catchphrase.

GENJI
I won't, though I might steal your wife.

Laughter.

TONOCHUJO (*Mildly irked.*)
O, I can see that it's going to be one of those nights.
But seriously, Genji –

GENJI
I was serious.

TONOCHUJO (*Irked.*)
Seriously!
It's an honour to welcome you to *Perfect Ten.*
I know you do so much work for worthy causes,
So tell us, what's your nominated charity to be?

GENJI
The home for homeless mistresses' children.

Applause.

TONOCHUJO
What a generous guy! And I know it's something
That's close to your heart, this charity;
All those poor little bastards, quite literally!

44

So let's play 'build your babe'
For all those homeless mistresses' children!
You all know the rules.
Round one is 'Mother, Geisha, Whore'
The contestant is asked three questions,
For each correct reply
He receives twenty seconds building time.
Get all the questions right
And you have the full minute to build your *Perfect Ten*.
So Genji, are you ready?
'Now spin the wheel which way will it fall
Mother, Geisha or Whore?'
Mother, Awww!
First question, Genji,
You fall in love with a woman
Whom you realise looks like your mother.
What do you do?
Drop her, undergo analysis,
Or fuck her just for filthiness?

GENJI
Nothing. I'd do nothing for what it's worth.

TONOCHUJO
O?

Laughter.

GENJI
My mother died in childbirth.

Silence.

TONOCHUJO (*Unsure.*)

Yes, of course. I'm sorry to hear that.

I think he deserves twenty seconds does he not?

Silence.

Question two,

Spin the wheel, where will it fall;

Will it be Geisha or Whore?

It's Geisha!

Okaysha!

You are out with your friends,

The meal ends,

You fancy one of the Geisha's but

You fear she is underage, do you – ?

GENJI

What are you saying?

TONOCHUJO

The question that's written here –

GENJI

I mean what are you trying to imply?

Silence.

TONOCHUJO

Nothing. I just I, I, I…

If I could just read you the possible responses.

GENJI

But my intentions are always honourable.

Pause.

TONOCHUJO

I think we should give him the twenty seconds.

Applause.

Look, there's only one left, there are no more,
It's time for you to answer… (*With Audience.*) Whore!
You've wined her, you've dined her,
She's lying naked on the floor,
You're just about to whambangboomerang, when
She whispers 'Five thousand Yen!'
Do you A: pay –

GENJI

I never pay.

TONOCHUJO

Just let me read the question, please.
B: leave –

GENJI

But I never pay.

TONOCHUJO

C: pretend you didn't hear –

GENJI

I never carry any money,
I'm like royalty don't you see?

TONOCHUJO

But what about this dilemma?

GENJI

What dilemma? She'd give it to me for free.

Laughter.

TONOCHUJO

And for that answer, you've just earned yourself

Another twenty seconds,

Which gives you the full sixty seconds to 'build your babe'.

WOMAN brought in as doll upon trolley.

Ladies and gentlemen the dolly trolley!

Applause. Music. Tense silence.

Sixty seconds to build your babe starts now.

Clock starts ticking.

What's he going to go for first?

Hair. Well, after all

Can't have a perfect babe who's bald.

Now, what's next?

Breasts.

More like it.

That's what we want, we want tit!

So what's his perfect pair going to be?

Full, round, pert,

With hint of nipple just showing through the shirt?

O, O, O! Look at those!

I like a pair of tits that sit up and say herro!

Forty seconds left to go.

Now it's the bum, the business end of things.

What's it to be?

A small sweet succulent sixteen year old's ass,

Or great big bouncy booty,

On which you can rest your glass.

He's going for THE BIG ONE

With sexy sashay hips,

A beautiful deep harbour for to park his ship.

Now the lips,

Full and pouty,

Perfect for playing inny-outy.

Only ten seconds left and she's not nearly done.

What about eyes and ears and tongue?

What availeth a perfect ass, as the poet says,

If your babe be blind, deaf and dumb?

Eyes, dark;

Ears, small;

Tongue long, lubricious…

4 3 2 1 …

And he has built himself the perfect princess.

His perfect ten.

Exit TONOCHUJO. Applause. Music.

Scene 11

GENJI and WOMAN find themselves alone. GENJI takes her for a ride on his bicycle. They are happy.

GENJI

Because of one chance meeting by the wayside,

The flower now opens in the evening dew.

GENJI's servant opens door of limousine. GENJI and WOMAN enter car. Music. Champagne bottle and drinks.

GENJI moves to sit next to WOMAN, she moves seat. Servant brakes and WOMAN falls onto GENJI's lap. GENJI smiles.

Exit limousine, enter motel. The MOTEL OWNER is watching
Perfect Ten *on TV.*

MOTEL OWNER
Room 4.

GENJI opens bedroom door. Two men are performing sexual
acts.

GENJI
Room 4 occupied.

MOTEL OWNER
Room 3.

Enter room, seedy noises heard from other rooms.

WOMAN opens window. Bird sounds are heard.

WOMAN
Such a desolate and deserted place,
The gardens overgrown,
The hedges and grass, a dull monotone of snot green,
Even the pond is choked with weeds.
How depressing!

GENJI
But such is the price of fame,
The lengths one must go to to avoid observation.

WOMAN
Let us hope whatever wicked spirits live here, pass us by.

GENJI's mobile rings.

GENJI
Hello? Yes, no this is he.

O it's you darling, yes, I see…
I know I'm not there because I'm here…
Otherwise engaged…
Work.
No need to sound so enraged…
Later, when I'm home…
I'll see you then.
Yes, I am alone.
Now, if you don't mind, darling,
(*Going to hang up.*) I'm in the middle –
I beg your pardon?…
You are?
That's wonderful…
Yes, we will.
No, don't start now on your own,
We'll open one when I get home…

GENJI offers WOMAN a glass of champagne.

To me! I'm to be a dad again.
My second. Another boy
I shall father only men.

   WOMAN (*Devastated.*)
Congratulations. Well done.
Now I really think I should be gone.

WOMAN makes to leave but is stopped by GENJI.

As masked characters GENJI and WOMAN dance, drink, embrace and make love.

The WOMAN becomes a Hannya, an evil spirit. The Hannya drives GENJI off and kills Evening Faces.

Exit Hannya.

GENJI holds the dead Evening Faces.

GENJI
Evening Faces, what spirit has possessed you?
Don't leave me, Evening Faces –
Evening Faces, don't do this,
Don't do this to me.

Exit GENJI with corpse of Evening Faces.

Scene 12

The Consultation Room.

PSYCHIATRIST
So Evening Faces died?

WOMAN nods.

So now I can speak to Yumi?

WOMAN
I told you, I am Evening Faces.

PSYCHIATRIST
But Evening Faces is dead.

WOMAN
Yes.

PSYCHIATRIST
So I'm talking to a dead person?

WOMAN
Is that so strange?

PSYCHIATRIST
Not as strange as it once was.
Do you know why you are here?

WOMAN
Because four people died.

Scene 13

The Observation Room.

PROSECUTOR, CHIEF OF POLICE and PSYCHIATRIST under siege from reporters. Pizzas are delivered.

PROSECUTOR (*Reading newspaper headlines.*)
The Office Lady Murderer!
You had no right to go to the press with what we know.

CHIEF OF POLICE
It is in the public's interest to be informed
The investigation is progressing,
That the police force is not just messing
When it comes to serious crime, concerned
With only overtime and job security –

PROSECUTOR
Meanwhile the station is besieged by journalists,
We can't go home, see our loved ones,
Or even our families.

CHIEF OF POLICE
Excuse me, but I ordered pepperoni.

PROSECUTOR (*To PSYCHIATRIST.*)
What's that one you've got there?

PSYCHIATRIST
Chicken.

PROSECUTOR
I distinctly asked for anchovy.

PSYCHIATRIST (*Smells his pizza.*)
Here.

PROSECUTOR
You?

PSYCHIATRIST
Vegetarian.

CHIEF OF POLICE
Stands to reason.

They swap pizzas.

PROSECUTOR
Right gentlemen, is that us?

PSYCHIATRIST
What about the chicken?

PROSECUTOR
What about it? The chicken, is superfluous.

They eat.

So?

   CHIEF OF POLICE
So?

Pause. They eat.

So Doctor, are you any nearer?

   PROSECUTOR
Yes Doctor, please is the case becoming clearer?

   PSYCHIATRIST
Can I ask you a question, Your Honour, Inspector?
Do you think that a person wronged
Can conjure a hatred so profound,
That their unconscious, or spirit or soul,
Call it what you will, moves beyond
The perpetrator's mortal frame
To revenge the ill?

   CHIEF OF POLICE
What?

   PROSECUTOR
You mean possession?

   CHIEF OF POLICE
Possession? Is that the best you've got?

   PROSECUTOR
You mean like the case of Wakaranai,
The Emperor's favourite Samurai,
Who, when he found the Emperor had slept with his wife,
Took his own life by Hara Kiri.
He disembowelled himself ritually

There in front of the Emperor.
His best friend then beheaded him.
But, as his head rolled up to the Emperor's throne,
The lips still twitched,
Cursing the Emperor and his line.
The Emperor himself died some time soon after
Of causes unidentified.

CHIEF OF POLICE
Why do you look so mystified?
It's just like when you decapitate a chicken,
It runs around flapping
As if nothing much has happened,
But it soon keels over, hits the ground.
Its simply a muscle spasm.
Or do you expect me to believe
The chicken is so consumed
By hatred of the farmer,
Its headless corpse is temporarily possessed,
In order to exact revenge?

PROSECUTOR
We are discussing human beings here, Inspector.

CHIEF OF POLICE
We are behaving like headless chickens, Your Honour.

PSYCHIATRIST
The chicken pizza.

PROSECUTOR
What?

PSYCHIATRIST
The fourth pizza.

CHIEF OF POLICE
Another breakthrough, Doctor?

PSYCHIATRIST
She said she knew that four people died.

CHIEF OF POLICE
She did? Why was I not notified?
It shows she knows.

PSYCHIATRIST
She knows because you told her so.
But she said four, not two. You told her two.
Why would she say four?

CHIEF OF POLICE
Perhaps it's not the only time she's done it.
Perhaps she's killed more.

PSYCHIATRIST
She did not admit to killing anyone.

CHIEF OF POLICE
It is tantamount to an admission, therefore
A knowledge of who she is and what she's done –

PSYCHIATRIST
But her understanding –

CHIEF OF POLICE
To hell with her understanding!
We have established her legal identity;

Finger prints, records of her dentistry –

PROSECUTOR
She must understand who she is
If she's to be held responsible.
If not she'll plead diminished responsibility.
Doctor, does she understand who she is?

PSYCHIATRIST
Yes, but who she understands herself to be
Changes from one session to the next.

CHIEF OF POLICE
Well I too can be very different people.
Come Saturday you'll find me
On the banks of Lake Kawaguchi,
Work and family cares all left behind,
On my own, gazing into the clear water, I am
Serene,
A soul at peace and calm of mind.
But come Monday,
When I'm stuck in a traffic jam,
And the kids are fighting in the back,
And the wife is on at me yak, yak, yak;
How I don't make enough money,
How she needs a new dress,
How I'm a bitter disappointment to her,
How she couldn't care less
About the pressure that I'm under,
My blood boils, I see red.
I take out my gun and shoot her dead,
Through the yakking mouth.
Now are you saying I can go to court and plead

That this man wasn't really me?
That I am a peaceful fisherman, you see,
Fishing for fish on the shores of Kawaguchi.

   PROSECUTOR
But at the time of your hypothetical crime
You are in your right mind, Inspector
You understand your legal identity.
However, Doctor,
We have only one more week before we must charge her.
And in light of the pressure we are under
Let me make the terms of your assessment clear;
Does the suspect understand who she is?
And did she understand who she was when she committed
  this crime –?

PROSECUTOR's mobile rings.

   PROSECUTOR
Excuse me –
(*On phone.*) No, I haven't told her yet.
No, don't rush me, don't rush me.

*The PSYCHIATRIST and the CHIEF OF POLICE look at
him.*

   PROSECUTOR
I'll talk to her tonight, I must go. Yes.
(*To PSYCHIATRIST.*) Six more days, doctor.
And we cannot hang the Emperor's Mistress.

Scene 14

The Consultation Room. PSYCHIATRIST and WOMAN. The WOMAN rocks. Silence.

Scene 15

The Consultation Room. PSYCHIATRIST and WOMAN. The WOMAN cries, the PSYCHIATRIST attempts to comfort her. Silence.

Scene 16

The Consultation Room. PSYCHIATRIST and WOMAN. The WOMAN hurls a stool in anger. The PSYCHIATRIST attempts to calm her down.

Scene 17

The Consultation Room. PSYCHIATRIST and WOMAN, they are laughing.

Scene 18

The Consultation Room. PSYCHIATRIST and WOMAN.

WOMAN
A dilemma for you, my friend.
Some weeks ago my wife
Informs me she's pregnant once again.
In spite of her cold heart, our remote relations,
I am delighted, proud, what's more,

She's sure she'll have another boy.
However, I am then informed
By the Lady Rokujo,
Who I've been seeing of late,
A man needs some warmth
When his wife is made of ice,
Well she tells me that she finds herself in a similar state.
You know Rokujo?

PSYCHIATRIST
No, tell me.

WOMAN
Older, small, striking,
I would have thought she was smarter than that,
I would have thought she took more care.
What was she thinking?
Has she no concern for my position?
But she says she loves me, besides,
She says it's her last chance to have a child.

PSYCHIATRIST
I'd really like to meet this Lady Rokujo.

WOMAN
What about me?
I cannot leave my wife, that's clear.

Scene 19

*The Consultation Room. PSYCHIATRIST and WOMAN.
WOMAN paces, takes PSYCHIATRIST's pencil, tries first to cut
wrists, then throws it away. Silence.*

Scene 20

The Consultation Room. WOMAN constructs a shrine.

WOMAN
Jewel,
My jewel which never turns away,
You live at the bottom of the sea,
Stolen by the Dragon Queen.

Scene 21

The Consultation Room.

WOMAN
I'll leave her, Rokujo,
She's always been cold.
I'll leave her next year.
If you do this for me,
We'll go away and start afresh, I swear.
We'll start a business together.
I'll be there for you, trust me,
In this world and the next.
Next year.

PSYCHIATRIST
Is Lady Rokujo there?

WOMAN
Not now, she's a bit upset.

Scene 22

The Consultation Room.

WOMAN
His distance is a measure of my sorrow.
Why did he not call?
He must call me, he must call me tomorrow.

Scene 23

The Consultation Room.

WOMAN
Where's my lighter?
What have I done with my lighter?
What have I done?

WOMAN imagines she has burnt her hand. She panics.
PSYCHIATRIST turns off tape-recorder.

PSYCHIATRIST
Yumi? How did you burn your hand?

WOMAN smiles.

Who are you today?

WOMAN
I am the happiest woman in the world.
He's going to leave her, he's going to marry me.

PSYCHIATRIST
Lady Rokujo?

Scene 24

Enter PROSECUTOR and CHIEF OF POLICE.

Interrogation Room.

PROSECUTOR
Yumi,
Let us tell you about the death penalty:
In this state, when one is sentenced to death,
One is held alone, in a cell;
No visits, no company, no telephone.
Nor is one, nor one's lawyer, nor one's family
Told when the day shall be.
So, every morning at five o'clock,
The prisoner must await the knock:
Is that breakfast or is that death?

WOMAN (*Feeling her tummy.*)
I felt it, I felt it. It's true! It's true!
After I lost the first I thought I was through,
Too late, my last chance gone.
I'm sorry gentlemen, I'd love to chat on,
But I must dress myself for the Kamo Festival.

PROSECUTOR
For up to seven years, alone in their cell,
The condemned must live like that –

WOMAN
And Genji's captaining a team in the games.

CHIEF OF POLICE
And then, when the day eventually comes.

WOMAN
He asked me and not his wife to attend.

CHIEF OF POLICE
It happens so fast.

WOMAN
He's going to leave her. He's told her at last,
I'm sure.

CHIEF OF POLICE
The papers signed, you're taken to the room –

WOMAN
Last night. He sent me a message.

CHIEF OF POLICE
Without ceremony –

WOMAN
And actually, gentlemen, between ourselves, I hope –
No, I dare not say!

CHIEF OF POLICE
So fast, so fast that is but for the final act –

WOMAN
Yes, in fact, I'm sure he's going to propose to me there.

CHIEF OF POLICE
The last one we hanged took half an hour
To kick and thrash himself to death upon the rope,
His body –

WOMAN
Look what I've written on my fan.

CHIEF OF POLICE
– had to be cremated,
It was so bruised and battered when he'd finally done.

WOMAN
'You and me forever.'

CHIEF OF POLICE
Sign this statement, admit responsibility –

PROSECUTOR
I'll see that you just get life.

WOMAN
You and me.

The Consultation Room.

PSYCHIATRIST
Yumi?

PROSECUTOR
One last session Doctor, one.
Then you must make your report.
The public demand justice,
The public are outraged.

Scene 25

The Kamo Festival.

GENJI (*Reading fan.*)
'You and me forever.'

WOMAN
It's written on my heart.

GENJI
And I shall return the favour, my dear Rokujo.

(*He writes.*)
'Never sundered, never torn apart'

WOMAN
Your wife, Lady Aoi,

AOI'S MEN
Since she had given birth to their first boy,
Seldom ventured into public with her husband.
And, her advanced state of pregnancy
Only added to her reluctance to venture beyond the palace
  gates.

ROKUJO'S MEN
But her servants and her friends all begged her:
'Come to the Kamo Festival.'

AOI'S MEN
And so Lady Aoi relented. She would, after all,
And unbeknownst to him,
Join her husband at the entertainment.

ROKUJO'S MEN
The sun was already high when they set forth.

AOI'S MEN
But the road was too crowded to let her procession pass.

ROKUJO'S MEN

So her men commenced clearing the road, until at last
Only two palm frond-carriages remained –

AOI'S MEN

Her's –

ROKUJO'S MEN

And Rokujo's.

AOI'S MEN

Out of the way for the Lady Aoi.

ROKUJO'S MEN

Who do you think you are talking to boy?
My mistress isn't someone you push out of the way.

AOI'S MEN

Who are you to tell us who we can push and can't?

ROKUJO'S MEN

Who are you who thinks you can supplant
My mistress's position? Don't you know who she is?

Pause.

AOI'S MEN

No, I don't know who your mistress is.

The carriages crash. ROKUJO's carriage falls to the ground

GENJI

Lady Rokujo, I must introduce you
To my wife Lady Aoi.

AOI

Pleased to meet you.

GENJI

She is my assistant, at work.

And this is my son Kazu.

WOMAN

Pleased to meet you Kazu too.

AOI

Kazu has just started school.

WOMAN

How nice!

AOI

He's in the gifted and talented class.

WOMAN

Fantastic.

AOI

And the baseball team, he's captain, just like his father.

WOMAN

How nice!

Now if you don't mind, I've had rather –

AOI

O, I felt it! I felt it just now!

WOMAN

I beg your pardon?

AOI

You cannot keep a good man down!

I'm pregnant yet again.

I just felt my baby move around.

The feeling, it tickles, it's quite funny.

Feel it, feel my tummy!

GENJI

Feel my wife's tummy, Rokujo, do!

WOMAN feels AOI's stomach. AOI goes to sit. WOMAN passes fan to GENJI.

WOMAN

You and me forever.

GENJI (*Shows fan's other side to WOMAN.*)

Never sundered, never torn apart.

GENJI goes to AOI.

WOMAN

Don't turn away from me,

Don't break my heart.

You said you'd leave her, not me.

Don't turn away from me my jewel.

WOMAN telephones GENJI.

GENJI going to pick up phone, AOI gets there first.

I'll get rid of it, just like I did the last,

I have decided to –

AOI

Who are you?

WOMAN hangs up. AOI phones her back.

WOMAN
Genji?

AOI
Who are you?

Actions and words are repeated several times. Telephones ring constantly.

GENJI
Okay! Okay! Okay!
I'll tell you who she is.
She's Yumi, Yumi Yamanaka,
You met her at the Company's Sports Day,
My PA.
We've been having an affair for the last two years.
You can't say it surprises you.
And please, please, please spare me the tears.

AOI
Bitch! You knew he was married.

WOMAN
I'm sorry, I thought you knew
He told me that he told you
I'm so sorry

These lines are repeated. Silence.

WOMAN performs abortion.

AOI phones ROKUJO.

WOMAN
Genji?

AOI
You are good for nothing, bitch,
But scraping babies from your womb.

WOMAN as ROKUJO becomes Hannya.

AOI heavily pregnant is possessed by the spirit of the Hannya.

GENJI
Who are you?
What spirit are you who has possessed my wife?
Identify yourself.

WOMAN
'You and me forever'.

AOI dies.

GENJI
Rokujo! What have you done?

Scene 26

Consultation Room.

PSYCHIATRIST
So Rokujo's spirit possessed Aoi and Aoi died?

Pause.

But you did not possess Sasaki's wife, Yumi,
And Sasaki's wife, she did not die.

She gave birth to a second child.

What possessed you, Yumi?
What possessed you to do it?

WOMAN picks up chair and rocks it.

 WOMAN
I am a heart that is full of hate,
I am like a bush that has no root,
I am the firefly's flash and flicker in the dark,
Then I am gone.
My life fades like the dew from the leaf.
My love can never be restored,
Not even in a dream.
It is a gleam glinting up
From the deep, deep waters of the past.

 PSYCHIATRIST
What are you doing?

*WOMAN appears to enact the murder of the two Sasaki children
as her statement is read.*

Scene 27

On the steps of the Police Station to the assembled press.

 CHIEF OF POLICE
'In the morning Sasaki leaves the apartment with his wife,
she drops him to the train station. I am watching from a car
parked opposite as I have watched each morning for the
past month, since her calls became too much to bear. The
two children I know are still asleep inside.

PROSECUTOR

'I have only seven minutes. I take the paraffin canister from the car, enter the building and go up to his apartment. I have a spare key. I am careful when I open the door not to leave fingerprints on the handle.

CHIEF OF POLICE

'I pour the paraffin around the living room and light a cigarette, but I cannot start a fire with it.

PROSECUTOR

'There are some envelopes on the table, I try to light a fire with them in vain. I see a child in the doorway, I hear a baby crying.

CHIEF OF POLICE

'The crying grows louder and louder. I listen to the baby crying. I am struck by the sound. So commonplace, and yet to me it is a knife cutting me here, just below my breast. I look down and see –

PROSECUTOR

'That the handkerchief I hold has caught fire.

CHIEF OF POLICE

'I run in panic and drop both lighter and handkerchief –

PROSECUTOR

'A sudden blast of burning air –

CHIEF OF POLICE

'I am blown away outside of the apartment.

PROSECUTOR

'I almost faint.

CHIEF OF POLICE

'I pick myself up as best as I am able –

PROSECUTOR

'And run away.'

Scene 28

The trial is heard as the execution chamber is prepared.

CHIEF OF POLICE

I am happy to confirm that we have charged Miss Yumi Yamanaka of Fuchu City for the murder of the Sasaki children. We are confident that we have the right person.

PROSECUTOR

I ask you once again, Doctor, does the defendant know who she is?

Pause.

PSYCHIATRIST

Yes. But –

PROSECUTOR

And has she demonstrated awareness of the crime that has been committed?

PSYCHIATRIST

Yes, but –

PROSECUTOR

And does she admit to a role in this crime?

PSYCHIATRIST

She demonstrates awareness of the crime, and admits to causing the death of four children, but –

PROSECUTOR

Thank you.

PSYCHIATRIST

But I believe responsibility, in clinical terms –

PROSECUTOR

The terms of reference are clear, doctor –

PSCYCHIATRIST

The question remains who she believed herself to be when she committed this act –

PROSECUTOR

– and in light of the evidence before me, I have no alternative –

CHIEF OF POLICE

A victory for justice. A victory for the truth.

WOMAN is hanged.

Scene 29

Consultation Room. PSYCHIATRIST listens to the following on his tape recorder.

PSYCHIATRIST

Please sit down Yumi. Do you know why you are here?

WOMAN

I killed four children.

PSYCHIATRIST
You killed two children not four, Yumi.

WOMAN
I killed four children.

PSYCHIATRIST
Why do you insist on four? Who are the other two?

The PSYCHIATRIST goes to the hanged body and takes her down. The PSYCHIATRIST and the WOMAN dive under the sea.

Scene 30

Under the sea, they swim searching for lost treasure. The PSYCHIATRIST leads WOMAN to the red ribbon that was her aborted child. She gathers it to herself. The PSYCHIATRIST takes one end. It resembles an umbilical. The PSYCHIATRIST resembles her lost child. She is reunited with her lost child. She is at peace. The umbilical is cut to release the PSYCHIATRIST. WOMAN remains on the bottom of the ocean as the PSYCHIATRIST resurfaces and gasps for air.

The End.